How to Dazzle at

Information Technology

Ann Goodwin

Brilliant Publications

Contents

Introduction

How to Dazzle at Information Technology contains over 40 photocopiable ideas for use with KS3 students. However, many of them could also be used with year 10 and 11 students who are studying for RSA CLAIT. They are practice tasks which presuppose that students have the knowledge and skills required to use the various programs.

The first few worksheets are general and are designed to provide students with an insight into computers and component parts.

The drawing tasks are based on the program Paint. They cover drawing with shapes, line and curves, and freehand drawing with the pencil tool. The tasks require the student to copy and paste, fill, spray and flip. The worksheet entitled 'Plan your ideal bedroom' may also be used in conjunction with Maths work.

The word processing tasks cover inputting and editing text, changing the style and size of the font, using a spellchecker, using the cut and paste and recall facilities, changing line spacing and margins, adding borders, using find and replace, templates, word art, wrapping with text and working in columns.

The spreadsheet tasks introduce rows, columns and cells. They require students to format text and understand formulas. The worksheets include the four computation operations and look at using charts and finding averages. The students are also asked to sort data in order, replicate cells and alter column widths. The final spreadsheet task asks the students to make predictions. Group discussion may help the students understand the implications of budgeting.

The database tasks give the students practice in understanding how and why databases are used. They are asked to use fields and records to search and sort by more than one criterion and they are asked to print specified fields from selected records.

In the worksheets covering desktop publishing the students are asked to prepare page layout and use existing templates. They are asked to work in columns, centre and justify text and use different fonts. They are also asked to import clipart and draw pictures.

The author acknowledges that students with learning difficulties may find some of the worksheets difficult. However, with many information technology classes being taught as mixed ability groups, it is suggested that the teacher may wish to organize student partnerships that would support each other.

It is important that the teacher emphasizes the need to read all the instructions before starting. Most worksheets require the students to think through and plan before they begin to work on the computer.

How to use this book

The following worksheets are designed to supplement any information technology activities you pursue in the classroom. They are intended to add to your students' knowledge of drawing packages, word processing, spreadsheets, databases and desktop publishing The author has undertaken to ensure that all the tasks can be performed on any suitable package, although a few are specific to Microsoft Word.

It is not the author's intention that students complete all the worksheets in the book, rather that the worksheets be used flexibly. The book provides a bank of resources that will meet students needs as they arise. However, a few of the activities do require the student to re-open a task from a previous worksheet. Where this is the case it is stated on the worksheet.

The worksheets have been written in a way that encourages students to work things out for themselves. Some worksheets are a bit of a challenge and students may wish to work with a partner. Where this is the case it is stated on the worksheet. It is also useful to bear in mind that working in pairs is often desirable for students with learning difficulties. Extension tasks – **Extra's** – have been provided for quicker or more able students. Teachers may also like to use the ideas in the Extras to create further worksheets.

The author has designed the worksheets so that they can be completed within a one hour lesson, although some will need prior research to be undertaken.

He's surfing the net again!

Computer components

Complete this paragraph by filling in the blanks. Choose from these words:

components   **hardware**   **computer**

> A PC is not a single unit. A typical PC consists of several basic parts, or
> _____ , that work together. These physical components of a
> _____ system are referred to as hardware. Generally, you
> can think of the _____ as any part of the computer that you can
> see or touch.

Computer systems generally include the following components.

A system unit
containing disk drives, memory
chips, and a microprocessor chip.

A monitor (or screen)
so that you can see what you are
doing as you work.

A keyboard and mouse
for entering commands and data
(information).

A printer
for transferring your work to paper.

The system unit is the central part of the computer. Any devices that are
attached to the system unit are considered **peripheral**.

Task   Draw lines to match the words with the correct picture.

Printer

Mouse

Monitor

Computer

Keyboard

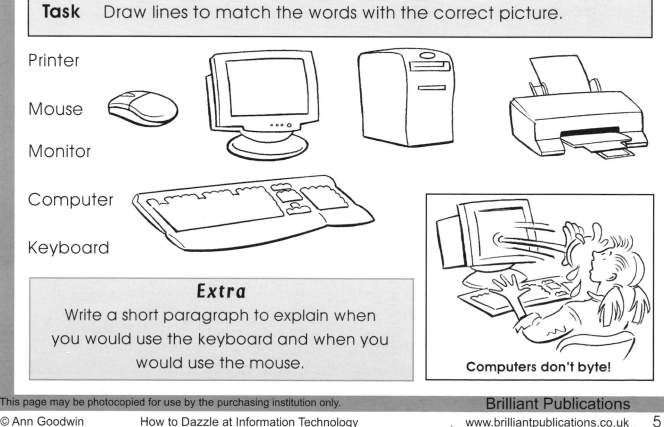

Extra
Write a short paragraph to explain when
you would use the keyboard and when you
would use the mouse.

Computers don't byte!

Brilliant Publications

How computers work

The computer works with information called **data**. Data refers to any information that is entered in the computer. For example, data can be the text of a letter, numbers in a spreadsheet, or a graphic image (picture).

You use your computer's hardware and software to perform a cycle of four basic activities. **Input** is information, or data, that flows into the computer. Input devices convert the data to a format the microprocessor chip can recognize. The computer then **processes** the data. The microprocessor chip interprets and executes the instructions. **Output** is the information that flows out of the computer. Information processed by the microprocessor chip is sent to an output or storage device. Output devices convert the computer language into a format you can work with, for example a printout or a picture on the screen. **Storage** is another basic function of the computer system. Information that will be used later can be transferred to a storage device, such as a disk drive.

Task   Write underneath each device whether it is used for **input**, **output**, **storage** or **processing**.

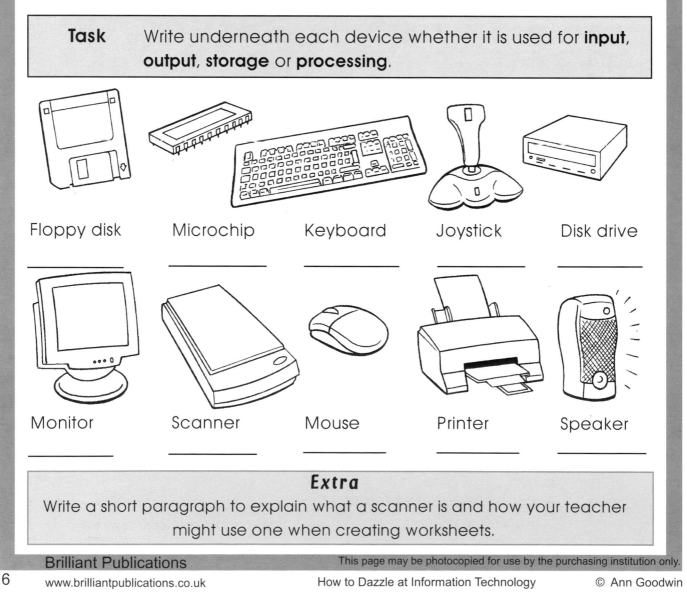

Floppy disk	Microchip	Keyboard	Joystick	Disk drive

Monitor	Scanner	Mouse	Printer	Speaker

Extra
Write a short paragraph to explain what a scanner is and how your teacher might use one when creating worksheets.

Brilliant Publications

How to Dazzle at Information Technology   © Ann Goodwin

Understanding a network

Most schools and colleges have a **network** of computers. This means that there is one main computer that makes all the other computers work.

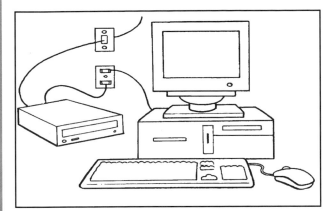 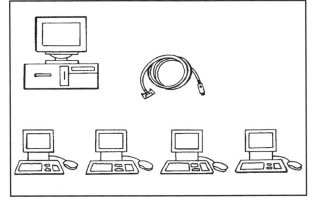

The main computer is called a **server**. All the other computers are called **workstations**. The server is usually in a different room from the workstations. They are linked together by cable that goes around the school.

Task

Why do you think the main computer is called a server? _____
_____

What would happen if the *server* was switched off? _____
_____

How many computers are on your school's network? _____

Complete the diagram to show the computer network at your school.

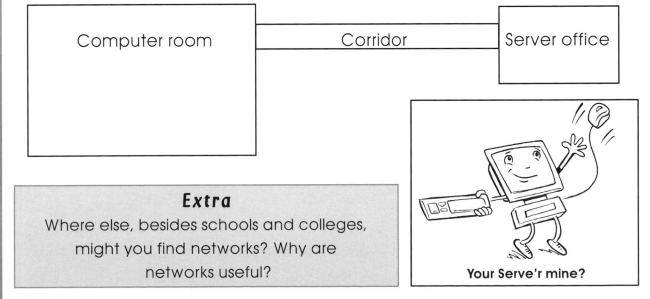

| Computer room | Corridor | Server office |

Extra

Where else, besides schools and colleges, might you find networks? Why are networks useful?

Your Serve'r mine?

© Ann Goodwin   How to Dazzle at Information Technology   **Brilliant Publications**   www.brilliantpublications.co.uk

Logging on to a network

A school network is divided into three areas.

Applications: This is where all the programs that we use are stored. This area can be used by both staff and students.

Users: students This is the area where you will save your work.

Users: staff This is where staff will save their work.

Getting into your area is called **logging on**.

You will need to log on to your own **user area** to find the **applications** you want to use and to **load** and **save** your work. The work you save is called a **file**. You will need to have a **user ID** and a **password** that is only for you. This area is then specially for you, so that you can save your work.

Task 1

Where will your teacher save any work? _____

_____

Where will you save your work? _____

_____

What does the word **applications** mean ? _____

_____

It is important that you remember your user ID and password, so that you can use the system again.

Task 2

Draw two pictures/logos that represent the programs in the applications you have used.

Extra

Find out how your teacher can use the network to make sure that all the students in your form have the same document on their own screen.

Don't forget your password!

Brilliant Publications

How to Dazzle at Information Technology   © Ann Goodwin

Looking at the keyboard

Finding your way around the keyboard will help to speed up your work.

Task 1
Press the letter a. Now press the Cap Lock key and type the same letter key. What happens? _____

_____

Task 2
Press the number 3 key. Now press the Cap Lock key and type the same number key. What happens? _____

_____

Task 3

Now hold the shift key ⬆ down with your right hand and press the number 3 key. Do this for any of the other numbers across the top of the keyboard. What does the shift key do? _____

_____

Next type in your teacher's name. Press the tab key ➔| once. Now type your name. Press the tab key again and type your friend's name. Press the ↵ enter key. Now type the same names again. Remember to press your tab key. What does the tab key do? _____

_____

Extra
Find out what the following keys do:

Insert   **Home**   **Page Up**   **Delete**   **End**   **Page Down**

Brilliant Publications

How to Dazzle at Information Technology   www.brilliantpublications.co.uk

Looking at hardware

Shown below are some monitors. What are they used for?

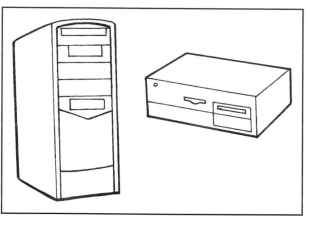

These are computers. Which type of computer does your school use?

Above is a keyboard. What is the number pad for? _____

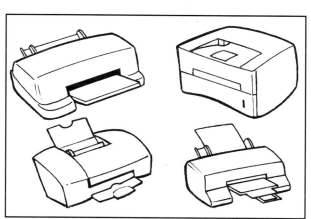

Above are printers. They can be dot matrix, laser or cartridge. What printer does your school use?

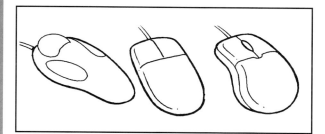

Above are some computer **mice**. Some have three buttons and some have two. Which type of mouse do you use? _____

When do you use the mouse?

Extra
Find out what other IT hardware your school has. What is it used for?

'Hey Barnie, my Laptop's got a Notepad!'

How to Dazzle at Information Technology   © Ann Goodwin

Looking at software

Software is the term used for the programs that we install on our computers. Different programs do different tasks.

Word processing is a program for writing.

Task 1

Think of five things that people might want to write using a wordprocessor. The first one is done for you.

1. A letter
2. _____
3. _____
4. _____
5. _____

How can a word processor make a writer's job easier?

A **spreadsheet**, sometimes called a worksheet, works with numbers.

Task 2

Find five things that people might want to use a spreadsheet for. The first one is done for you.

1. Working out how much pocket money you spend.
2. _____
3. _____
4. _____
5. _____

Find five things that you can do on a spreadsheet. The first one is done for you.

1. Add up a column of figures.
2. _____
3. _____
4. _____
5. _____

A **database** is a type of filing system.
When might your teacher want to use a database?

_____
_____

Extra

Find out what other software your school uses and why it is used. If you are able to you might discover some interesting software in the school office.

Don't bite off more than you can chew!

Fun with drawing packages

Most computers have some sort of drawing package. You can use drawing packages to draw your own pictures by using shapes and pencils.

Task 1

Create a monster:

    Draw three squares, two rectangles and one ellipse.

    Draw ears with the pencil.

    Colour in two of the squares by using the paint fill.

    Colour in the ellipse by using the paint spray.

    Give your monster a name and put it above your monster.

Print a copy. REMEMBER if you don't have access to a colour printer your squares must not be next to each other.

Task 2

Draw your own logo.

Your local council has decided to clean up the river that runs through   your neighbourhood. The council would like to make the area attractive to walkers and families but it would also like to encourage wildlife, especially river plants, animals and fish.

Create a logo to advertise this environmental problem. The logo will be used on all letterheads, posters and leaflets. The same logo will be used on stickers and T-shirts to be sold to raise money to support this venture.

Using the drawing facilities, duplicate part of your design using the flip or rotate facility.

Print a copy of your design.

Extra

Create a picture using only lines and curves. You may use the paint spray to enhance your picture.

Create a chessboard

Task

Before you can attempt this task you need to find out how many squares a chessboard has.

Work out how many squares you will need across the page and down the page.

Work out what size squares you can use to make the correct number of squares fit onto an A4 page.

Using the square shape, draw one that is the correct size.

Copy and paste this square until you have the correct number of squares.

Using the paint fill facility, colour each square to match the design of a chessboard.

REMEMBER to make sure that you put your name at the top of your work before you print. If you have completed this task correctly everyone's printout should look the same.

Example:

Extra

Using the same number of squares as you used on the chessboard, create a snakes and ladders game. Number each square. Use the appropriate drawing facility to draw the snakes and the ladders.

Plan your ideal bedroom

You may want to work with a partner to do this task. You will need a furniture catalogue that gives the sizes of the furniture.

Task   Design your ideal bedroom and print out a plan view of it. (The size of your bedroom will need to fit onto a sheet of A4 landscape.)

Use the furniture catalogue to help you decide what you would like in your bedroom.

Using a pencil and paper, draw a rough plan of where you would put the furniture.

Make sure that the measurements of the furniture are roughly scaled down to fit the size of the paper.

Using the appropriate drawing facilities in the drawing package, copy your rough plan onto the screen.

Label your furniture.

REMEMBER you will need to note where the windows and the door are situated.

Add a title to your drawing.

Print a copy of your room plan.

'Nice bedroom design, Sophie, but where's the bed?'

Extra
Using the same method, design a house or bungalow. REMEMBER it is important where rooms go. It is no good putting the dining room next to the bathroom.

How to Dazzle at Information Technology   © Ann Goodwin

Word processing

Word processing is brilliant for writing. It means that you can write something, save it, print it, check it, change it, and print it again. It means that you don't have to write **everything** all over again – only the bits you want to change.

You will need to ask your teacher how to get into the program you are going to use. Then begin by typing the following:

Orange & Lemon Fizz

INGREDIENTS
Makes 1 litre
1 1emon
250 ml orange squash
1 bottle lemonade
Ice cubes

EQUIPMENT
Lemon squezer
Small sharp knife
Jug
Glasses

Cut lemon inhalf, and cut one half into 3 – 4 slices.
Squeeze juice from other half, place in jug.
Add orage squash and ice cubes.
Pour on lemonade.
Float lemon slices on top and serve.

Save your work. REMEMBER you must give your file a name that will remind you what your work is about. Call this one **Orange Fizz.**
Print a copy. Exit the program.

Extra
Find out how to save your work if you want to use it on another computer that is not on the network.

Brilliant Publications

Editing your work

Editing or changing your work is very easy. Get into the word processing package. Open your file called **Orange Fizz**. Place the cursor after the first 'e' in the word **sque zer** and add another **e**. Now check the rest of your document for spelling and make corrections. (If you have a spellcheck on your program, use this.)

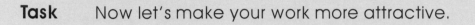

Task Now let's make your work more attractive.

■ First highlight the words **Orange & Lemon Fizz**.

To do this, take the cursor with the mouse to the first letter **O**.

Hold the left button down.

Drag across to the last letter **Z**. See how the words are highlighted.

■ Now with the mouse take the pointer to Times New Roman in the list box. Click on the down arrow to the right of the box and find a font that you like. Now take the mouse to the next box ⏹ 12 and change the size of the font to 18.

■ Change the style and size of font for the words **INGREDIENTS** and **EQUIPMENT**. *(These words need to be smaller than the title, but larger than the text.)*

Extra

Type out a nursery rhyme, such as Baa Baa Black Sheep. Underline the title and put it in bold. Now centre the text. Put a border around the rhyme.

'I said EDIT, not eat it!'

Cut and paste

Copy out the following few paragraphs and save your work as **Incy wincy spider**. Unfortunately, it seems to be a bit mixed up. Put the lines in the correct order.

> Down came the rain
> And washed the spider out.
>
> Incy wincy spider
> Went climbing up again.
>
> Out came the sun
> And dried up the rain.
>
> Incy wincy spider
> Climbed up the spout.

REMEMBER to highlight the text you want to move and then use cut and paste or just drag it to the correct place.

Tasks

- Now change the spacing to 'double line' and make the text justified, so that both the left and right hand edges of the text are in a straight line.

- Now change the spelling of a few words to give the following mistakes. Change **climbing** to **climing**, **dried** to **dryed**, **washed** to **woshed**. Using the spellchecker, change them back to correct spelling.

Extra

Choose another poem or write a story yourself. Mix it up and then ask a friend to sort it into the correct order.

Brilliant Publications

Changing margins and paragraphs

A student has written a paragraph about making and breaking friends, for your school magazine. Your job is to input the data ready for printing.

- Type out the following and save it as **Friends**.

Making friends is always fun. You begin by finding out about the other person: their name, their age and what they like doing. You can tell them what you want them to know. You don't have to tell them anything that you don't want them to know. It's a new start.

As time goes by, you find out more about your friend. They may have annoying habits. They may not have told you the truth. There are a great number of reasons why disagreements may happen but when they do they are very upsetting. You feel hurt and let down.

However, this is part of learning. Each time this happens to you, you will be more choosey in your choice of friends. You will have a better idea about what to look for – what you want from a friend. So don't think of this as a bad experience. Think of it as another step in growing up.

****

Task

The editor has asked you to:

Give this article a title.

Make the title bold and centre it.

Reduce both the left and right hand margins by 25mm.

Justify the right hand margin.

Save and print a copy.

Extra

Open the document *Friends*. Add your own thoughts to this article. Delete any that you don't agree with. Format this text into two columns and add a picture.

Find and replace

The headteacher has asked you to send the following letter to four sets of parents.

Tasks

Copy the original. Insert the date for the awards evening as next Friday. Save the letter as **Award**, and print it out.

Using Find and replace, change the names of the parents and their child as appropriate. Send a letter to each of the other parents, who are:

Mr and Mrs Sheldon – their son is Paul
Mr and Mrs Kendrick – their daughter is Marie
Mr and Mrs Dennison – their daughter is Karen

Using the same method, change *his* to *her* and *son* to *daughter* as appropriate. Print a copy of each letter.

Charters High School
High Street
Cheestone
Worcestershire
WV5 7EU
Phone 0127-555-1234
Fax 0127-555-9876

INSERT DATE 2000
Dear Mr and Mrs Jones

I wish to congratulate your son Philip on his recent award as Achiever of the Year. This is tangible proof of his ability to work hard throughout the year. Philip continues to study hard and has overcome any difficulties he had initially. My staff and I would like to express our pride in his achievements both in his academic subjects and in his sporting activities.

I would like to invite you to attend our awards evening on   *DATE*   at 7 pm and for refreshments in my study afterwards. I look forward to seeing you again.

Yours sincerely

Horace E Williams
Headteacher

Extra

Using the original letter, change the award to be given to *100% Attendance Award*. The two students to receive this award are: Melanie Johnson and John Howard. Amend the letter as appropriate. Print a copy of each.

We need a certificate

The head of PE would like a new design made for the certificates to be awarded to the winners of the sports events.

> **Task**
>
> Design three different certificates:
> one for first place
> one for second place
> one for third place

◆ Use a template for certificates from your desktop publishing package and follow the instructions given.

◆ Decide whether you want your certificate to be A4 portrait, A4 landscape or A5.

◆ You must leave a space for the headteacher's signature and the date.

◆ You will need to insert the event and the competitor's name on each certificate.

Make sure that the certificate is attractive and, if you insert a picture, make sure that it is appropriate .

Extra
Using the templates on your program, create a sports day newsletter to report on the events of the day. You can use clipart or drawings to illustrate your newsletter.

Wrapping with text

A local recording studio heard your school band and choir perform some of the songs the students have written. Most of the songs are about being a teenager in a modern world. They have agreed to make a CD with the school band and choir. The head of music has decided to have a competition to find the best design for the CD cover. He has set certain guidelines for you to follow.

Task	Design the CD cover.

◆ The CD cover must have a picture on it.

◆ It must show the school name.

◆ The title for the CD must reflect the type of music on the CD.

◆ The text must be wrapped around the picture.

◆ A list of the songs must be shown.

◆ Use WordArt if you have the facility.

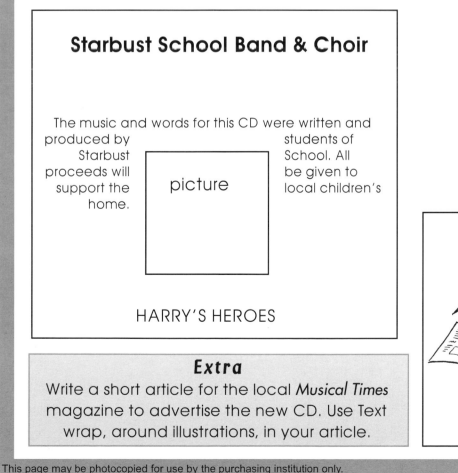

Starbust School Band & Choir

The music and words for this CD were written and produced by Starbust proceeds will support the home.
picture
students of School. All be given to local children's

HARRY'S HEROES

He just can't get the hang of this wrapping!

Extra
Write a short article for the local *Musical Times* magazine to advertise the new CD. Use Text wrap, around illustrations, in your article.

Working in columns

Your school is to produce a weekly newsletter. Each week students and staff will write articles on a variety of subjects, which will include:

- ○ Star students
- ○ Forthcoming events
- ○ Your letters
- ● Competitions
- ● Environmental issues

Task Set up a template for the magazine using a word processing package.

The magazine will need a name and the date at the top.

Each article will need a headline.

The page must be set in three columns.

Example:

THE NOTTSVILLE TIMES

20 May 2000

Student success es

Forthcoming events

Your letters

Competitions

Environmental issues

Save and print a copy of your template for future use.

Extra

Ask your friends to join you in collecting data for your magazine.
Type the data onto your saved template. Insert appropriate pictures.

How to Dazzle at Information Technology

Creating your own letterhead

You can only do this worksheet if you are able to use WordArt.

> **Task**   Type the following company heading: **Clowns R Us**.

Add or edit a special text effect.

You can do this by using the WordArt button on the Drawing toolbar. You can create shadowed, skewed, rotated, or stretched text, as well as text that has been fitted to predefined shapes. As a special text effect is a drawing object, you can also use buttons on the Drawing toolbar to change the effect $^3/_4$ for example to fill a text effect, with a picture. The WordArt button replaces the WordArt program, although you'll still have the WordArt program on your computer if you have an earlier Microsoft program that contains it $^3/_4$ such as Office, Works or Publisher 95.

Keep in mind that a special text effect is a drawing object and is not treated as text. You won't be able to see the text effect in outline view or check its spelling as you would with ordinary text.

To add a special text effect:

- On the Drawing toolbar, click WordArt .
- Click the special effect you want, and then click OK.
- In the Edit WordArt Text dialogue box, type the text you want to for mat, select any other options you want, and then click OK.
- To add effects to the text, or change them, use the buttons on the WordArt and Drawing toolbars.
- Now type in a fictitious address.
- Add a company logo from clipart.

Extra
Create a new letterhead but make sure that the address is centred across the page. Add a footer to your letter stating the VAT registration number 458 6988 00. Print a copy with your name and today's date on the top.

It's a special effect!

Spreadsheets

Spreadsheets are brilliant for Maths work. You can add, subtract, divide and multiply large numbers. You can create graphs and charts.

Task 1 Get used to typing information into the cells.
Step
1. Take the cursor to row 1 column A
2. Type in XXXXX
3. Take the cursor to row 6 column D
4. Type in XXXXX
5. Take the cursor to row 9 column G
6. Type in XXXXX
7. Highlight and press delete (Del).

Task 2 You are now going to design a booking form for a holiday rota at work. Copy the following.

Holidays

	MAY	JUNE	JULY	AUG	SEPT
Julie	XXXXX		XXXXX		
Abida		XXXXX	XXXXX		
Shazia	XXXXX			XXXXX	
Adeel					
Stephen					

Adeel and Stephen are the newest members of staff and have to choose their holiday dates after everyone else. No more than two members of staff can be on holiday at any one time. Presuming that each member of staff takes two weeks off at a time. Choose two weeks holiday for Adeel and Stephen and type in 5 X.

Type your name and form at the bottom and print a copy.

Extra

Create a register of students in your class. Add a column for each month of the year and complete days of the month when students' birthdays occur.

How to Dazzle at Information Technology   © Ann Goodwin

Using a spreadsheet

The following is a sample of a student's weekly expenditure.

Task
Calculate the total spending for each day, then the total for each week. Then calculate separately the amount of money spent each week on comics, sweets, bus fares and dinners. Save your work.

Weekly expenditure

	Sun	Mon	Tues	Wed	Thurs	Fri	Sat	Weekly total
Comics, papers	20	30		28	35	20	20	
Sweets	50	30	65	37	53	70	68	
Bus fares		20	20	20	20	20	37	
Dinners		1.20	1.15	1.41	1.15	1.63	2.53	
Daily total	70	81.2	86.15	86.41	109.15	111.63	127.53	672.07

■ Write down the formula for finding the total amount spent on Sunday.

■ Write down the formula for finding the total amount spent on Wednesday.

■ Write down the formula for calculating the total amount spent during the week on bus fares.

■ Write down the formula for calculating the total amount spent on dinners.

The above answers don't make any sense, as no-one would spend that amount on those items. The problem was that we forgot to tell the programme the correct currency we are using.

■ Write down the instructions for formatting figures into currency.

■ Explain what would happen if you forgot to format the cells into British currency?

Save your work and print a copy. Make sure that your name and today's date are on the top of your work. (REMEMBER that means you must insert a row.)

Extra
Discover what sorts of things need to be paid each week to run a house and complete a weekly household budget.

Sorting into order

The following is a class list with results in Maths and English examinations.

Task

Print a copy of the class list in alphabetical order.

Work out and print a copy of the class list of the English results, (highest first).

Work out and print a copy of the class list of the Maths results (lowest first).

Examination results

Surname	First name	English mark	Maths mark
Jones	Melanie	81	78
Martin	Jodie	78	65
Kaur	Sukjinder	56	33
Allwood	James	45	74
Carter	John	76	36
Partridge	Lesley	83	58
Williams	Niah	33	62
Davidson	Paul	57	30
Benton	Heather	66	54
Grainger	Mark	72	70
Petersen	Julie	59	56
Evans	Katie	73	75
Jones	Jacqui	51	63
Featherstone	Terri	44	80

■ Calculate the average mark for English.

■ Calculate the average mark for Maths.

■ Print a copy of your results.

Extra
Create a graph showing the English and Maths results for this class.

Totals and averages

Copy the following table into your spreadsheet program.

Students' examination marks

Name	Database	Spreadsheet	Word processing	Graphics	Total	Average
A Cooper	69	68	82	45		
S Chauhan	36	72	56	36		
J Matthews	75	45	73	64		
P Newman	56	32	49	78		
L Patel	61	64	51	49		
J Smith	67	78	62	51		
Total						
Average						

Tasks

■ Calculate the total of the students' Database marks.

■ Using the copy formula calculate the marks for Spreadsheets, Word processing and Graphics.

■ Put your name and today's date at the top of your work and print a copy of your results. Print a further copy showing the formulas.

■ Calculate A Cooper's total marks.

■ Using the copy formulas calculate the other students' total marks.

■ Calculate the average marks for each subject and the average marks for each student.

■ Print a copy showing the formula and one copy showing the marks.

Extra

Ask each student in your class which month their birthday is in. Create a spreadsheet showing the number of student's birthdays in each month. Create a pie chart to show your results.

Brilliant Publications

© Ann Goodwin   How to Dazzle at Information Technology   www.brilliantpublications.co.uk

Using multiplication

Your teacher wishes to place an order for stock to be used by her students for the following term. Type the following information onto a new spreadsheet. REMEMBER to format all prices into currency.

Stock code	Description	Price each	Quantity	Total price
1863A	A4 White paper	£2.30	6	
2761B	A4 Green paper	£2.60	3	
7831	Black ballpoint	£1.99	12	
4789	Blue ballpoint	£1.99	12	
7885	Black printer cartridge	£5.99	6	
7889	Colour printer cartridge	£6.50	6	
5789C	Mouse	£10.98	3	
SUBTOTAL				
VAT				
TOTAL				

Save the worksheet as **Stock Order.**

Tasks

- Multiply the quantity required by the cost of A4 White paper.
- Copy the formula down to the next 6 cells.
- Add the subtotal and enter into cell E9.
- Work out the VAT that is required (VAT is at 17.5%).
- Add the sub total and the VAT to arrive at the total.
- Insert a row and type in your name and today's date.
- Save your work and print a copy.
- Your teacher has realized that she has forgotten to order lined paper. Insert a row after stock code 2761B and enter 12 reams of A4 lined paper stock code 7821X, at £2.45 per ream. Your total should change automatically.

Extra

Create a new sheet for the next term's stock order. The teacher has to order 6 more reams of lined paper, 8 reams of A4 white paper and 3 reams of green paper. She also needs 12 boxes of pencils at £2.20 per box, stock code 4598C. She has an allowance of £960. Assuming she will spend a further £80 on stock in the third term, how much money has she got left to buy textbooks?

Multiplication and division

Aisha, James and Sehmi have been given the task of organizing the food for the end of term party. They have also been asked to let everyone know how much they will need to contribute towards the food. There are 27 students in the form.

Type the following information onto a spreadsheet. REMEMBER to format **cost** and **total** into currency. (You may need to use Word wrap on cells where there is more than one line of text.)

Item	No. required	Cost	Description	Total of each item
Loaves	10	.46	each	
Margarine	4	.43	each	
Ham	3	.51	per 100gms	
Cheese	4	.61	per 100gms	
Tomatoes	2	1.10	per 450gms	
Crisps	4	1.15	per large bag	
Nuts	3	1.36	per large bag	
Pepsi	12	.97	per bottle	
Choc. mini rolls	12	1.23	per packet	
Total				
Amount due each person				

Tasks You will now need to calculate:
- the total cost of each item using the multiplication function.
- the total cost of all the food using the multiplication function.
- the amount that each person will need to contribute towards the food by dividing the total cost by the number of students.

Which cells will change if you alter the amount of margarine required from 4 tubs to 2?
Print copies of your spreadsheet showing the formulas and totals.

Extra

Create a spreadsheet for a child's fifth birthday party. REMEMBER to research the type of food they would like and the amount of food they would need.
There will be 33 children at the party.
Print out copies showing totals and formulas.

Replicating entries

Your teacher has organized a trip to France and has asked you to enter the following details on to a spreadsheet. REMEMBER format the figures into currency.

Tasks

- Each student paid £50 deposit.
- Copy the cell containing Marie Smith's deposit for £50.
- Sue and Paul have paid the same amounts as Marie. Copy these cells down.
- Kelly and Darren have paid the same amount as Wayne. Copy these cells down.
- The next seven students have paid the same amount as Navdeep. Copy these cells down.
- Emily, Kate, Terri and James have paid the same amount as Charlie. Copy these cells down.
- Create a formula to give a total for the deposits paid.
- Create a formula for the total amount paid in week one. Copy this formula for each week.
- Create a formula to give a total for Marie. Copy this formula for each student.
- Save under **Holiday Finance** and print a copy.
- Sort the data into alphabetical order, and print a copy showing the formulas.

MONEY COLLECTED FOR HOLIDAY IN FRANCE

Cost per student
£120

SNAME	FNAME	DEPOSIT	WEEK 1	WEEK 2	WEEK 3	WEEK 4	WEEK 5	TOTAL
Smith	Marie	50	20	10	10	10	20	
Johnson	Paul		20					
Barker	Sue		20					
Colley	Wayne		10	10	10	20	20	
Evans	Kelly							
Evans	Darren							
Birdit	Navdeep		20	10	10	10	10	
Martin	Heather		20					
White	Amy		20					
Slattery	Caroline		20					
Dagleish	Peter		20					
Barry	Jodie		20					
Mahoney	Ben		20					
Ghil	Suresh		20					
Williams	Charlie		10	10	10	10	20	
Rees	Emily		10					
Terry	Kate		10					
McNeall	Terri		10					
Thomas	James		10					
TOTAL								

How to Dazzle at Information Technology   © Ann Goodwin

Using a spreadsheet to predict

This worksheet is quite hard. You will need to think carefully about how to create your spreadsheet. It may help if you work with a partner.

Task Katie is a college student studying Business Studies. She gets a small grant and has a part-time job to help pay for her books and equipment and still allow a little left over to pay for some leisure activities.

Create a spreadsheet to predict how much Katie can spend on herself each week during the term. There are 13 weeks in one term.

- ❐ She earns £52.63 per week.

- ❐ She has a grant of £326 per term.

- ❐ In week 1 of the term she had to buy books costing £60.33,

- ❐ She also had to buy paper, pens and folders costing £21.97.

- ❐ Each week she gives her mum £25 towards housekeeping.

REMEMBER you will need to use addition, subtraction, multiplication and division.

Extra

There are only 3 termly grant payments. Create a spreadsheet to predict how much Katie will need to save for the 13 weeks' holiday not covered by a grant. Katie has the opportunity to earn an extra £25 per week during the holidays. She will have to spend the same amount each term on books and equipment.

'When I were nipper, my mom only had two crusts of bread and a lump of coal to feed us lot of nine kids all week!'

Spreadsheet crossword puzzle

CLUES:

Across

2. To choose or highlight means to...
4. You place data going across the page in a ...
5. It means to change or to alter.
6. You add, subtract, divide and...
8. D_ _ _ _ _ _ point.
11. Data that is not letters.
13. To open a file.
16. You must do this to use your work again.
17. Diagrams of your results.
19. Letters or words but not numbers.
20. Symbols that represent the steps in a calculation.
21. Tags that identifiy the x and y-axis.

Down

1. You place data going downwards in a ...
2. Another word for the total when numbers are added together.
3. It also unlocks a door.
7. Information in pictorial form.
9. Where rows and columns meet.
10. Plus means ...
12. You can spend or save it.
14. You sit at this.
15. To get out of a program you _ _ _ _ it.
18. Numbers added together give you the...
19. The key that takes you from one cell to the next one.

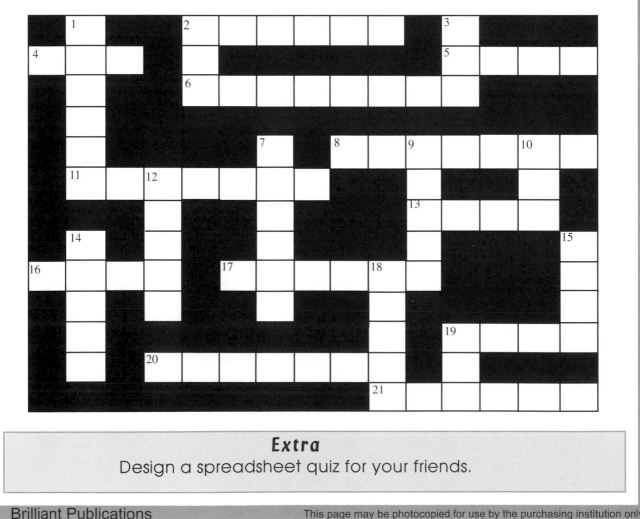

Extra
Design a spreadsheet quiz for your friends.

How to Dazzle at Information Technology   © Ann Goodwin

Create a database

In the past your school will have kept a record book to show all the students' examination results. With new technology many schools now keep all records on a database.

- Give three reasons why this method of storing examination results is better for the school.

- How would these examination results have been stored in the past?

- What is a field in a database?

- What is a record?.

Task	Create a database for the following information.

Examination results

Students	English % mark	Maths % mark
Melanie Jones	81	78
Jodie Martin	78	65
Sukjinder Kaur	56	33
James Allwood	45	74
John Carter	76	36
Lesley Partridge	83	58
Niah Williams	33	62
Paul Davidson	57	30
Heather Benton	66	54
Mark Grainger	72	70
Julie Petersen	59	56
Katie Evans	73	75
Jacqui Jones	51	63
Terri Featherstone	44	80

Save this file under the name **Exam Results**. Print a copy. REMEMBER you will need your name on your printout.

Extra
Write a short report to show the reasons why teachers would find this type of record-keeping more useful.

Using a database for analysis

Open the file called **Exam Results** that you saved from the previous task.

> **Tasks**
> - Sort the database to print a copy of the students in alphabetical order.
> - Paul Davidson has left the school. Please delete his record.
> - Mark Grainger has changed his name and now wishes to be called Mark Johnson. Please amend his record.
> - Sort the file to show English examination results in ascending order and print a copy.
> - Search the database for all students with more than 60 % in Maths and print a copy.
> - Print a copy of the student with the highest mark for Maths.
> - Print a copy of the student with the highest mark for English.

Complete the blanks in the following sentences.

To _____ a record means that you add a new record to the database.

To _____ a record means that you remove a record from the database.

To _____ a record means that you change some data in it.

A database is formed by creating the required number of _____ and entering _____ .

Records can be sorted _____ and _____ _____ .

> **Extra**
> Add two fields to your database. One for Science results and one for Geography results. Enter imaginary marks for each student. Print a copy of the results in descending numeriaclalorder.

Brilliant Publications

This page may be photocopied for use by the purchasing institution only.

34   www.brilliantpublications.co.uk   How to Dazzle at Information Technology   © Ann Goodwin

Which film?

Task Create a database for the following information. Be careful when setting up your database, that the *type* of each field allows you to sort and search.

Film title	Year of release	Classification	Age limit	Length of film (mins)
Rebecca	1940	Thriller	PG	126
How to Make anAmerican Quilt	1995	Romance	12	112
Fly Away Home	1996	Drama	U	103
Gotti	1996	Drama	18	117
The Crow: City of Angels	1996	Horror	18	91
Macho Max	1995	Drama	18	91
The Last Hard Men	1976	Western	18	93
Sweet Charity	1969	Musical	PG	142
Father's Day	1997	Comedy	12	94
Wings of the Dove	1997	Drama	15	100
Breakout	1975	Thriller	15	93
Sirens	1994	Comedy	U	90
Africa Screams	1949	Comedy	U	73
Pete's Dragon	1977	Fantasy	U	123
West Side Story	1961	Musical	U	146
Town on Trial	1956	Thriller	12	92
George of the Jungle	1997	Comedy	U	87
Sink the Bismark	1960	War	U	93
Pony Express	1953	Western	U	97
Contagious	1997	Thriller	15	87
Money Train	1995	Comedy	18	105

Save your work under the filename **Films**. Print a copy of this data.

REMEMBER to put your name at the top.

Extra
Explain why it is important to say whether the field is alphanumeric or numeric.

Choosing the right film

In this task you are going to choose the right films for viewers. Open your file **Films** from the previous task. REMEMBER you may need to search on more than one field. You must put your name and the date at the top of each printout.

Martha is a 52-year-old lady who likes to watch films which she calls 'The Oldies'. She doesn't like horror films, or westerns for any of the modern films that have funny sense of humour. She doesn't have to worry about how long the films are.

Task   Create a search to find films that Martha would like to watch.
Print out a list of these films.

Pete is Martha's grandson and he is coming to stay for the school holidays. Martha would like to get a few videos for him to watch during his stay. Pete is 12 years old.

Task   Create a search to find films suitable for Pete.
Print out a list of these films.

Martha's grand-daughter, Selina, will be spending the weekend with her grandmother. She is 19 and on the way home from university. She wants a break from her studies and loves to watch any film from the nineties. As she also wants to visit friends she doesn't want to sit in front of the television for more than 1 3/4 hours.

Task   Create a search for films suitable for Selina. Create a search for films suitable for Denver. Print out a list of these films.

Selina's boyfriend, Denver, will be visiting her at her grandmother's and loves to watch horror films, westerns osr comedies. He doesn't mind how long he sits infront of the television.

Task   Create a search for films suitable for Denver. Print out a list of these films.

Extra
Create your own database about CDs. Make sure that you have at least four fields. Then ask your friends to search the records for three different criteria.

'Wicked!'

How to Dazzle at Information Technology   © Ann Goodwin

Who does what?

Your local sports and leisure centre has recently decided to create a database of the activities that members use.

Task Enter the following details into a database. You will need to set your Page-set-up to landscape. REMEMBER some fields need to be numerical.

Member no.	Main leisure interest	Sex	Age	Times per week	Average £ per year
1	Karate	M	25	2.6	34.5
2	Swimming	M	41	3	56.8
3	Tennis	F	32	1.5	23.5
4	Squash	M	28	4.3	64.8
5	Swimming	M	46	3.7	45.5
6	Weight training	F	19	2.1	49.6
7	Tennis	F	17	3.2	38.5
8	Squash	M	29	2	39.6
9	Karate	M	12	4.6	23.7
10	Weight training	M	24	4.1	56.2
11	Squash	F	26	2.3	70.5
12	Tennis	F	31	4.3	61.3
13	Swimming	F	15	3.5	23.5
14	Swimming	F	16	3.5	23.5

Save this as **Leisure Centre**.

Format the membership number column so that the numbers are aligned to the left. Format the column for the average times used per week to read as integers. Format the column for the amount paid per year to British currency.

Save and print a copy. Print a copy of each of the following details.

Find the average time per week that members spend playing tennis. Which members use the swimming pool? Print their membership numbers and the average number of times per week that they swim.

Extra

Open the database **Leisure Centre** and add four new members. One plays tennis four times per week and pays £40.50 per year. He is 29. One 14 year old girl plays squash twice a week and pays £28 per year. How does this alter your results? Print a copy for each result.

Finding a holiday

Going on holiday is something we all look forward to. It is a time when the family relax and have fun together. However, finding the right holiday that suits all the family is a difficult process.

You will need ta holiday brochure for research.

Task	Set up a database of holidays suitable for a family of four (2 adults and 2 children).

The children are aged 8 and 11 years. The family don't really mind a self-catering holiday but would prefer half-board facilities. They do not want to take their holiday during term time. They wish to fly from Manchester, East Midlands or Gatwick airport. Mum and Dad would really appreciate some free time – so activities for the children would be welcome. They do not like to be on a plane for more than four hours and would like the resort to be under three hours coach journey from the destination airport. They do not wish to spend more than £800 (plus spending money) on the holiday.

- [ ] First decide which fields you want to create.
- [x] Refer to your holiday brochure and choose ten holidays to enter into your database.
- [ ] Save under **Holidays**
- [ ] Sort your holidays into alphabetical order by resort.
- [ ] Print a copy. REMEMBER to put your name at the top.
- [ ] Print a copy of the holidays that depart from Manchester airport.
- [ ] Select the most suitable holidays for the family.
- [ ] Print a copy of your choices based on the criteria above.

Extra
Recall your database **Holidays**. The family has decided to take the children's grandmother. She likes to sit on a beach and read. She also likes to watch the evening entertainment in the hotel.

Using desktop publishing

Desktop publishing is the type of program used by publishers of newspapers and magazines. Most programs have templates for different types of documents. If the program that you use has templates, choose one that would give you a letterhead.

Task 1

Choose the paper orientation as A4 portrait. Type your name at the top. Type your address underneath your name. Insert a picture. Save your work as **Letterhead**. Print a copy.

Task 2

Re-open your file called **Letterhead**. Type a letter to a friend from overseas, inviting him/her to come to stay with you during the school holidays. Save this letter as **Letter 1**. Print a copy. Close this file.

Task 3

Re-open your file called **Letterhead**. Type a letter to a magazine asking for help with a problem. Save this letter as **Letter 2**. Print a copy.

Extra

Find a template that is suitable for business cards. Make up the name and address of a company. Insert a company logo. Print yourself 6 business cards.

Create a poster

Task

Use a template in your desktop publishing package to create a poster to advertise your school's annual sports day.

- Your poster must be eye-catching.

- It must not have too much writing on it.

- It must give all the information.

- You may choose to use A4 landscape or A4 portrait

The date of the sports day is 7th June 2000.
The starting time is to be 1 pm with the last event at 3 pm. Some events may be held at the same time in different places.

The events will take place at the local sports field, in the gymnasium or in the swimming pool. The event will be opened by the famous footballer Roland Rich.

- You will need to decide whether to use landscape or portrait orientation.
- You will need to decide whether to use colours or whether black and white would be more effective.
- Do you want to add a border to your poster? Make sure that you do not make the borders too 'busy'.
- If you use clipart pictures make sure that they are appropriate .

Extra

Create a poster to advertise the sports day for display
in the local shops. How will it be different?

Brilliant Publications

This page may be photocopied for use by the purchasing institution only.

40   www.brilliantpublications.co.uk   How to Dazzle at Information Technology   © Ann Goodwin

Create a leaflet

Task
Your school wishes to produce a leaflet to show the programme of events for the annual sports day. This is to be a four-page leaflet. If your package gives you the facility to use A4 landscape that folds like a book, this is an effective size to use.

REMEMBER the leaflet must be attractive and informative.

The events to be held are as follows.

Events

1 – Yr 7 Long jump, Yr 8 Long jump, Yr 9 Long jump and Yr 10 Long jump.
2 – Yr 7 Girls Trampoline, Yr 8 Girls Trampoline, Yr 9 Girls Trampoline, Yr 10 Girls Trampoline.
3 – Yr 7 Boys Trampoline, Yr 8 Boys Trampoline, Yr 9 Boys Trampoline, Yr 10 Boys Trampoline.
4 – Yr 7 Girls 100 metre sprint, Yr 8 Girls 100 metre sprint, Yr 9 Girls 100 metre sprint, Yr 10 Girls 100 metre sprint.
5 – Yr 7 Boys 100 metre sprint, Yr 8 Boys 100 metre sprint, Yr 9 Boys 100 metre sprint, Yr 10 Boys 100 metre sprint.
6 – Yr 7 Girls Relay, Yr 8 Girls Relay, Yr 9 Girls Relay, Yr 10 Girls Relay.
7 – Yr 7 Boys Relay, Yr 8 Boys Relay, Yr 9 Boys Relay, Yr 10 Boys Relay.
8 – Yr 7 Girls 180 metres freestyle, Yr 8 Girls 180 metres Freestyle, Yr 9 Girls 180 metres freestyle, Yr 10 Girls 180 metres Freestyle.
9 – Yr 7 Girls Javelin, Yr 8 Girls Javelin, Yr 9 Girls Javelin, Yr 10 Girls Javelin.
10 – Yr 7 Boys Javelin, Yr 8 Boys Javelin, Yr 9 Boys Javelin, Yr 10 Boys Javelin,

Extra
The task shows only a sample of sports events held by school's. Research your own schools sports events and produce a leaflet to be used at your next sports day.

'Come on, jump to it!'

Brilliant Publications

Design a certificate

After the school's annual sports day the winners are normally presented with certificates to acknowledge their success.

Task Design three certificates, for the first, second and third in each event.

Choose A4 landscape as the page layout. REMEMBER you will need to include:

the place achieved in the event
the name of the event
the date of the sports day
the signature of the head of P.E.
the name of the school
a picture

It may look something like this:

Certificate

This is to certify that
Fred Smith
was first in
Year Nine Long jump
13th May 2000

Extra
Create a certificate for a student who has passed six grade A and three grade B, GCSE qualifications. This is to be recognised as an exceptional achievement for the student.

More chips anyone?

Writing a newsletter

Task   Write a newsletter using a suitable template from your desktop publishing program.

- Your newsletter is for your local youth club.

- Create a newsletter with three columns.

- Give your newsletter a name and make sure that it goes across the three columns.

- Add the date and price.

- Write your first story about a cycling outing that a group of club members went on. Give your story an appropriate headline. Insert a picture.

- The next story is a report on a group of local residents who are complaining about the noise from club members as they leave the club to go home. Give your story an appropriate headline. Write the story. Insert a picture.

- Save your newsletter under the name **Club News**. Print a copy.

Extra
Create a pop music magazine in two columns. Using the drawing features, create your own logo for the magazine. Ask other members of your form to each write a short article to be included in your first issue.

He's crashed!

This page may be photocopied for use by the purchasing institution only.

Brilliant Publications

© Ann Goodwin   How to Dazzle at Information Technology   www.brilliantpublications.co.uk   43

DTP wordsearch

There are 21 words connected with desktop publishing to find. REMEMBER to look across, down and from corner to corner. Some may also be back to front.

BOX	GUIDES	PAGE
CLIPART	HANDLES	PICTURES
CREATE	INSERT	PUBLICATION
DESKTOP	LINE	PUBLISHING
DRAW	OBJECT	TEXT
FRAME	ORIENTATION	WIZARD
GALLERY	OVAL	ZOOM

T	U	R	D	A	T	A	B	A	S	E	W	I	Z	D	R	A	Z	I	W
C	E	R	E	U	Y	W	I	O	P	M	N	Y	I	P	R	A	W	Z	V
B	N	X	Q	W	E	D	E	S	K	T	O	P	O	P	T	R	E	A	S
C	V	B	T	N	M	M	T	R	E	W	I	Z	E	I	O	P	U	M	I
W	R	T	Y	U	I	P	U	B	L	I	S	H	I	N	G	I	N	G	Y
H	D	E	K	P	Y	T	R	I	T	R	A	P	I	L	C	T	I	O	N
A	S	I	D	O	R	I	E	N	T	A	T	I	O	N	F	G	W	H	J
N	L	N	Z	X	C	V	B	N	M	Q	W	E	R	T	Y	A	U	I	F
D	T	S	O	Y	R	E	L	L	A	G	P	D	E	R	R	S	K	R	T
L	K	E	J	P	U	B	I	H	G	F	O	D	S	D	A	Q	A	W	E
E	C	R	E	E	T	I	N	G	H	G	B	D	D	E	R	M	T	O	E
S	E	T	P	I	C	T	U	R	E	S	J	W	E	R	E	T	Y	I	H
Z	S	E	N	T	R	E	D	W	R	A	E	P	B	U	E	B	L	I	S
A	C	T	E	S	E	D	I	U	G	I	C	O	O	N	P	G	A	P	D
F	R	N	M	M	E	O	B	J	K	R	T	C	X	T	L	L	A	N	A
C	I	V	B	M	K	Z	O	O	M	M	O	Z	O	V	A	C	D	P	E
L	A	S	T	P	U	B	L	I	C	A	T	I	O	N	V	V	C	B	R
C	R	E	W	T	Y	U	P	U	B	F	O	T	N	B	O	V	E	R	P
W	I	N	R	T	Y	F	O	P	R	E	M	N	B	F	C	D	T	H	S
C	L	I	O	E	W	E	T	A	E	R	C	A	R	T	U	Y	B	R	C

Extra

There are two words that relate to IT, but not desktop publishing. Can you find them?

DTP quiz

Task How quickly can you answer these questions?

1. Who might use a desktop publishing package at work?

_____

_____

2. Name two ways to arrange the orientation of the paper.

_____

_____

3. What is meant by a **template**?

_____

_____

4. Name three templates that you can use from a desktop publishing package.

_____

_____

5. Explain how you would create a newsletter with three columns.

_____

_____

_____

_____

6. If you are creating a newsletter using a desktop publishing package, how can you put a picture in your work?

_____

_____

_____

_____

Extra
Collect three different types of advertising material.
Which templates you would use to set them up?

Brilliant Publications

Answers

Spreadsheet crossword puzzle from page 32

The completed crossword grid contains the following answers:

- 1 down: column
- 2 down: sum
- 2 across: select
- 3 down: k
- 4 across: row
- 5 across: edit
- 6 across: multiply
- 7 down: graphs
- 8 across: decimal
- 9 down: cell
- 10 down: load
- 11 across: numbers
- 12 down: money
- 13 down: total
- 14 down: table
- 15 down: exit
- 16 across: save
- 17 across: charts
- 19 across: text
- 20 across: formula
- 21 across: labels

DTP wordsearch from page 45

The wordsearch grid with words circled.

Glossary of computer terms

Task   Learn the spellings and their meanings of all the words below.

application – a progam that allows you to do something useful with your computer.

bit/byte – how the computer stores information, in binary; 8 bits to a byte

chip – interprets and executes instructions.

clipart – a picture that is already in the program, that you can choose to put in your work.

components – pieces of equipment that joined together make a working unit.

corridor – the link between the server and the computers.

crash – a system failure.

cursor – the black line or arrow on the screen that shows you where you are entering or editing.

data – information.

desktop publishing (dtp) – a program that allows you to put together text and pictures in a newspaper format.

disk drive – this is where the disk is put, for the computer to read or edit text.

document – pages that show the information you have inputted.

edit – to change or alter something in a document or file.

field – the cell or compartment in a database where details are stored, e.g. in a maths field your teacher may type in all the students, marks from a test.

file – a document holding information.

floppy disk – a soft disk that holds/stores the information from the computer.

font – the style or shape of letters.

hardware – the equipment that makes up a computer; the parts that can be touched.

icon – a picture on your screen that you click on, to make your computer do something.

input – any information that is put onto the computer.

joystick – the control lever that is used to move the direction of the cursor.

keyboard – the keypad attachment to the computer that allows you to type and give other instructions.

landscape – the long side of a piece of paper in a horizontal position.

load – to put in to, e.g. disk in drve.

logo – a picture or letters that represent the name of a company, e.g. the M for McDonald's.

log on – to put in your name and password.

menu – a list of 'pull down' options from which a user selects.

monitor – the screen you look at to see your work.

mouse – the hand controller with one two or three buttons to move the cursor.

network – a number of computers and other devices that are linked together, so that they can share information and programs provided by the server.

output – the information seen on the

Brilliant Publications

screen or a printout.

password – a set of numbers/letters that you type into the computer to prove your identity.

peripheral – a device or part of the computer that is attached to the system unit.

portrait – with the long side of a piece of paper in a vertical position.

printer – a device which, linked to the computer, prints out hard copy. Dot matrix, laser or cartridge types.

program – the software that allows you to do different tasks.

scanner – a device that is able to transfer an image from a photograph into a file on the computer.

server – the main computer that stores the programs that run the workstations.

software – programs that we install to do different tasks.

spreadsheet – an application on a program that allows you to add, subtract, divide or multiply.

storage – a device used for storing the information on your file e.g. disk drive.

system – a number of components that make up a working computer.

templates – a blank document design that gives the /layoutpattern, e.g. of a letterhead or a poster.

user – person using the computer.

word processor – a program designed for writing letters and reports.

workstation – a computer terminal or screen that is linked to a server.

wrapping – the command to make text flow around a picture.

'Hey cool. Check out this web, Marcia!'